a police wife devotional

by Kristen Linton

heelsandholster: a police wife devotional

Dedication

To my husband, Rick, for building with me a life I am proud to share with the world. Words cannot express how thankful I am for our adventure. You changed me.

To my children, Maverick and Leonidas, for bringing me joy each day. What a blessing it is to be your mom and watch you grow.

To my mom, Nancy, for teaching me selflessness and creativity. Every song I sing to our boys and meal I cook for my family I learned from you.

To Rick's mom, Zandra, for raising Rick to be a loyal, good person and for modeling resilience.

To Rick's dad, Rick, for raising Rick to be patient, brave, and a provider.

How to Read this Book

This book chronologically documents key growth for me as a police wife. You can read it from start to finish. Alternatively, you can read it based on the topic. This way, if you feel challenged on a specific topic, you can either jump right to it or come back to read it as you need. Following this page will be a table of contents in chronological order in addition to a table of topics.

Table of Contents

Introduction   9
1. New Love   11
2. Injured on Duty I   13
3. How my Officer Sees Things I   15
4. His Coworkers   19
5. Trauma   22
6. Engagement   26
7. Passion for the Job   30
8. Police Hate I   32
9. How my Officer Sees Things II   36
10. The Wedding   39
11. Newlyweds   43
12. Finances   47
13. Faithfulness   50
14. Always on Duty   53
15. How my Officer Sees Things III   59
16. Police Hate II   62
17. Injured on Duty II   64
18. How My Officer Sees Things IV   68
19. Motherhood I- Making a Baby   70
20. Wives Make Sacrifices Too   72
21. Communication   75
22. Bullets Found Where?   77
23. Motherhood II- Preparing for Childbirth   80
24. Motherhood III- Childbirth I   82

25. Hypervigilance I   86
26. Motherhood IV- The Baby Stage   89
27. Resentment   92
28. Loneliness   95
29. Motherhood V- Childbirth II   98
30. Concealed Carry   102
31. Prioritizing our Marriage   105
32. Hypervigilance II   108
33. Motherhood VI- Raising Children of a Police
Officer   110
34. Holidays   112
35. Mexican Restaurant   116
36. Finding Peace I   118
37. Injured on Duty III   120
38. Police Hate III   125
39. Motherhood VII- Choosing a School   129
40. The Toe that Broke the Kristen's Back   132
41. Finding Peace II   133
Conclusion   135
Other Resources   136

Table of Topics

Always on Duty	53
Communication	75
Concealed Carry	102
Engagement	26
Faithfulness	50
Finances	47
For a Good Laugh	
Bullets Found Where?	77
Mexican Restaurant	116
Toe that Broke Kristen's Back	132
Finding Peace	
I	118
II	133
His Coworkers	19
Holidays	112
How my Officer Sees Things	
I	15
II	36
III	59
IV	68
Hypervigilance	
I	86
II	108
Injured on Duty	
I	13

II	64
III	120
Loneliness	95
Motherhood	
I Making a Baby	70
II Preparing for Childbirth	80
III Childbirth I	82
IV The Baby Stage	89
V Childbirth II	98
VI Raising Children of Police	114
VII Choosing a School	129
New Love	11
Newlyweds	43
Passion for the Job	30
Police Hate	
I	32
II	62
III	125
Prioritizing our Marriage	105
Resentment	92
Trauma	22
Wedding	39
Wives Make Sacrifices Too	72

Introduction

I am a Catholic convert, vegetarian, raised by animal-loving hippies on a ranch in Hawaii and Las Vegas. I met my husband, Rick, who was raised by a traditional Mexican mom and veteran, police officer Dad in Las Vegas. We dated on and off, and both moved states for graduate school and careers. A decade after meeting, Rick and I got married in 2013. Rick has been a Los Angeles police officer on patrol, gang units, and other specialized units for 16 years. When this was written, we had been married for 9 years, and this book includes stories from the 19 years we have been together, from 2003 to 2022. We are blessed with two beautiful boys, Maverick and Leonidas. Thankfully, I have grown throughout my journey as a police wife.

At times, police wife life was lonely and isolating. I also experienced resentment. However, prayer, mindfulness activities, connecting with other wives, and homemaking are tools that empowered me to be resilient regardless of the challenges.

In this devotional, you will find 41 bible verses, stories, prayers, and jokes. I have been known for my police wife comedy on social media @heelsandholster. I hope this devotional brings you peace and hope, makes you laugh and feel less alone, and strengthens your marriage.

1. New Love

Proverbs 5:18-19

Let your fountain be blessed, and rejoice in the wife of your youth, a lovely deer, a graceful doe. Let her breasts fill you at all times with delight; be intoxicated always in her love.

How I Met My Officer

I was bored in biology class, sitting next to my friends, not understanding our instructor and nonchalant about what the instructor had to say. I was 17 in a college class, and my friends and I were a part of a community college high school program. Suddenly, my gaze caught this cute, blonde guy a couple rows behind me in a plain white T-shirt and jeans. He looked like a surfer boy. Little did I know that *I* would be the one to introduce him to surfing! I wrote him a note, "Dear Man in the White Shirt,…" which I passed to my friend, who then passed it to him. The man in the white shirt and I passed notes back and forth for the entire class period.

I learned barely anything about the Man in the White Shirt. When I asked him what he did for work, he said he pushed boxes around a warehouse. Later, I learned he helped people with disabilities in a day program. I told him I wanted to be a social worker, but I was working at American Eagle at the mall at the time.

The note ended with the Man in the White Shirt, Rick, asking me to "go out for caramels and lemonade." And the rest of our shenanigans for the next 19 years…are in this book, so keep reading!

Prayer

Lord God, let me always remember those simple, early days full of passion and excitement for my husband.

2. Injured on Duty I

Isaiah 40: 28-31

Have you not known? Have you not heard? The Lord is the everlasting God, the Creator of the ends of the earth. He does not faint or grow weary; his understanding is unsearchable. He gives power to the faint, and to him who has no might he increases strength. Even youths shall faint and be weary, and young men shall fall exhausted; but they who wait for the Lord shall renew their strength; they shall mount up with wings like eagles; they shall run and not be weary; they shall walk and not faint.

Rick's Dad

I was sitting at the table with Rick and his parents. The table décor was splashed with bright colors, including Mexican-themed salt and pepper shakers at the center. Rick's mom had made me a bean and cheese burrito while the rest of the family enjoyed a meat and pasta casserole-since I was vegetarian. Their family believed it was not a meal without meat, though they respected my choices.

Rick and his dad were quiet. Rick never talked much; he got this trait from his dad. Rick's mom, Zandra, and I filled the silence. She asked me about my plain black work shoes and described them as masculine. She was bold and asked if they were in style. I responded, "I guess so. I think they are just simple." Rick's dad did not hear me. So he rotated his head toward me to hear from one side. Later that night, Rick told me his dad, a retired Las Vegas police officer, had been shot in the head on duty at a domestic violence call when Rick was just a boy. Hence, he lost hearing in one ear.

Prayer

Heavenly Father, thank you for the heroes who face traumas as they protect communities. Today, I pray that our heroes feel the strength of our Lord as they survive traumas. I pray that those who feel weak may feel a renewed strength from our Lord. I pray that our officers are resilient. Let their injuries make them stronger. Please let them hear our gratitude for their service and sacrifices. Let our communities surround them with healing love and gratitude.

3. How My Officer Sees Things I

Romans 12:15

Be happy with those who are happy and weep with those who weep.

The Futon Store

Rick and I moved into a small 1-bedroom condo he bought. I was so excited to decorate it even though we were both broke college students.

I did not know the first thing about homemaking then. My mom had spoiled me by doing almost all the grocery shopping, even until I was in college. My home, growing up, was full of furniture we moved from Hawaii to Las Vegas with us, some of which was made by my grandfather. Most of the art on the walls also came from Hawaii, including art my family members had painted. Our home was spacious with Spanish-style tiles and an overall '70s vibe. My mom was not one to remodel much. She tended to our family by cooking dinner almost every night and taking care of the ranch animals we had in the backyard, including horses, chickens, and even turkeys. A fun fact about me is that I speak "turkey." When I laugh, they gobble. You might say it is a talent. We also had dogs, cats, and birds. Dogs were always my favorites. I could handle the calm, old ranch horses and chickens we had, but that was about it. I used to lie on the back of an old ranch horse we had named Mouse while he was in his stall; that was pretty much my speed.

While we appeared to live that country lifestyle, it was more of a hippie lifestyle, because we never ate any of our animals. Our free-range chickens lived full lives. We did eat the eggs they laid and shared them with neighbors and friends. Also, my parents never owned a gun. They had a baseball bat under their bed for protection, which I only ever saw *my mom* pick up when she heard something weird in front of the house.

Rick and I decided we would look for a futon for our living room if anyone wanted to stay with us. First, we went to a futon store. On walking in, Rick immediately got quiet. He acted especially weird. He was always quiet, so that was not the weird part. He followed me, walking around and checking out all the furniture, but neither of us got too excited about any of them and left.

As soon as we got in the car, Rick said, "I think that place is a front." I ignorantly asked, "What do you mean? Why?" He answered, "I don't know. You can just sense it. There weren't too many futons in there. I think it's a money front for something else."

Rick was not yet a police officer, but he was raised by one. He already saw the world through a different lens than I did.

Prayer

Jesus, I pray to ask that you help me to see things through my husband's eyes. I pray to be educated and informed about all my husband deals with as a law enforcement officer.

As I pray this, I wonder if that is my role. If this is not my role, I pray to be a good listening ear. I pray to have patience and understanding. I pray to see the world through my lens and help my husband see the good in the world on days he cannot.

I also pray to be open to adapting our lives in ways that make my husband's life easier and more peaceful without sacrificing my own peace, such as always sitting with my back to the front door in restaurants.

4. His Coworkers

1 Peter 3:8

Finally, all of you have unity of mind, sympathy, brotherly love, a tender heart, and a humble mind.

The Third Wheel

Though he did not talk to me much about it, Rick says probation was harder than the academy. The academy physically humbled him. He knew how to shoot and pass a written test, but he worked out with his friend, Res, who was also in the academy, before and after academy days to get into physical shape. According to Rick, Res had been a Marine before joining the police and was in incredible shape.

Rick's probation time seemed to be more about tough love and testing his psychological limits than anything. I was a Master's degree student in Chicago when Rick was in the academy. We had a long distance relationship, but I came to visit him during my winter and summer breaks.

One day, Rick and I were driving somewhere together. It was just us in the car, but Res was on the car phone. At first, he and Rick did some small talk, and then it was silent. Rick pulled over to a gas station and filled up while I sat there in the car. I figured he had hung up the phone since it was so silent, but when he got back in the car, he started talking to Res and making jokes with him on the phone again.

Even as a long-distance couple, Rick and I did not linger on the phone like that. This girl has got stuff to do, you know? It was *so* weird to me.

As a police wife, I have learned that, while Rick and I will go through many things together, his work partners have a unique bond that I cannot fully understand. When they get together, they joke so much that I cannot keep up; I feel like the third wheel. I have learned to encourage Rick's relationship with Res and his other partners. Sometimes, I feel like he needs to see his work partners if he has dealt with something that I just cannot relate with him on; that is okay. I serve my role in his life differently. I will be there when his career is over. Maybe some of his work partners will be in our lives, but maybe not.

While he is an officer, he needs them as other people who *get* exactly what he is going through.

Prayer

Lord, I pray my husband has solid, dependable partners and coworkers in law enforcement. I pray that their bond strengthens my husband. I pray my husband feels less alone due to his friendships with his coworkers. May they laugh together to recover from the stresses of their work. Lord, let them have his back and keep him safe.

5. Trauma

Psalm 34: 18-19

The Lord is near to the brokenhearted and saves the crushed in spirit.

Nightmares

Having dated on and off for almost a decade since we met in 2003, Rick and I were back together after I contacted him on an interview at a Los Angeles-based university. We reconnected for a dinner date after my day-long interview, and he met me in my hotel room. I was nervous because it had been a few years since I had seen him. When I opened the hotel room door, I saw it in his eyes. He had new wrinkles and bags under his eyes. Not the kind that made him look bad, though.

Isn't it almost annoying that men literally grow sexier with age?

We both had been through a lot since the last time we had seen each other. We had dated while I was getting my Master's degree in Chicago, but we had not reconnected during my PhD years in Arizona until that last semester when I had that interview. I am sure that I had more wrinkles, too. His own graduate school and police work had taken their toll on him. We were both older; this would be the last time we reconnected. The End.

Just kidding. It was the last time we reconnected because we were *finally* together for good after that. We both knew we were "the one" for each other. Rick was finally ready for marriage, which I had told him was important to me in the past. He wanted to be ready to be a provider and did not want to settle down until he could be confident in that role.

Not yet engaged but comfortable knowing that we were in this relationship for the long run, I was sleeping next to Rick in the room he rented from a fellow officer and friend in Los Angeles. I was a deep sleeper. Once my head hit the pillow, I was out like a rock. In the middle of the night, something woke me. I did not know where this weird noise was coming from. It was a worrying noise like a vibrating "uuuugghhhh" but in a humming repeated sound. I realized it was coming from Rick. I gently touched him and said "Rick" to see if that would get him out of his dream. It did not affect him at all, and the noise continued. With one hand, I pushed on his shoulder and said, "Rick, you're okay." He responded that time, breathed deeply, and thanked me. He seemed kind of lost in thought. Then we both went back to sleep. The next day, I asked Rick about it; he said it was a nightmare and did not want to talk about it. He said his roommate had woken him up from them before.

I have often woken Rick up from these nightmares over the years of our marriage. They do seem to happen more often when Rick has dealt with stress at work. I call them "PTSD [Post-Traumatic Stress Disorder] nightmares," and Rick does not argue with me.

Prayer

Heavenly Father, I pray to you to bring my husband peace. Leave those stressors of his workday at work. Empty those thoughts. Let his eyes and mind rest so he can sleep. Let him dream heavenly thoughts.

6. Engagement

Ecclesiastes 9:9

Enjoy life with the wife whom you love, all the days of your vain life that he has given you under the sun because that is your portion in life and in your toil at which you toil under the sun.

Cotton Candy Skies

Over the phone, Rick was planning his visit to see me in Hawaii for my birthday. He asked if I wanted to go out to eat with my friends and him for my birthday or just with him. The social butterfly in me said, "With friends and him."

Rick was a planner and the best with surprises. Prior to his visit, Rick got called to court on one of the days he was supposed to be in Hawaii with me. He was nervous about this one and tried to see if his partner could show up instead of him. We were both nervous as we both wanted to see each other. Finally, it all worked out, but this issue of the court getting in the way of things was just the beginning.

Rick made us reservations at Merriman's Honolulu right on Waikiki at sunset. The sunset had already started with a cotton candy sky when we arrived. Rick said, "I reserved that too," referring to the beautiful sunset. I cannot make any promises, but I am pretty sure I rolled my eyes and laughed. He was always so quick with responses and jokes!

Before being seated, a server asked us to wait at the bar. While we waited, someone came over to him and said, "Excuse me, sir, but you have a phone call."

Ya'll, these are *cell phone* days, so that was weird.

I waited at the bar while Rick went to "take a phone call." To this day, Rick will not tell me what that was about.

My friends arrived, and we all sat down to share a bottle of wine. Before our food arrived, Rick asked me if I wanted my presents. Of course, I did! Did he even have to ask? He handed me a heavy, rectangular box first. This part gets a little blurry between the tears running down my face and the wine, but what I opened was a scrapbook Rick made telling our story. I knew right away that something special was happening. Almost immediately, Rick was down on one knee beside me, asking me to marry him. I said…

Yes, of course! I was a mess of happy tears.

I felt like I needed a friend to stand up and yell, "My friend is getting married, and she dated the man for 10 years!" Yes, that was the second movie reference in this book. Can you tell we like movies?

Prayer

Dear God, bless us as we enter new beginnings in our relationship with responsibility and devotion for one another rather than other material things. Let us prioritize one another, our families, and the important people in our lives who support us to succeed.

In our unique lives as a law enforcement family, let me be reminded of the sacrifices we take as a family together. My husband will sacrifice his safety and time away from his family for his career. May I be reminded that he serves you, God, in this role. I sacrifice and serve you by taking on more responsibility at home while he works long hours. Give me a deep understanding and pride in this as we enter our marriage.

7. Passion for the Job

Galatians 6:9

Let us not lose heart in doing good, for in due time, we will reap if we do not grow weary.

"Just Give Me Five Good Years"

We were in Washington DC for the Top Cop Awards, where Rick was a nominee. He was not even sure what for, but we wanted to go to DC with his dad. We wanted to take advantage of going there, see the sights, and go to museums. I researched where all the museums were and got us tickets. Rick said he was impressed by how organized I was. Of course, I had changed from previous trips we had taken. When we were younger, I was more relaxed and didn't really know my way around.

While we were there, Rick reflected on his career. He loved his job and was proud of helping people and the community. I, on the other hand, wanted him to do some other kind of work. He was smart and was studying to get his doctorate in Psychology then. Concerned, I was scared he could get hurt.

He said, "Can you just give me 5 years? I just want 5 good years." It made me emotional. I felt his pull to serve, but I felt that it pulled him away from me. He knew that, and that is why he asked for just five years.

I said, "Okay," not actually knowing what I was getting myself into.

Prayer

Lord, do not let me have a timeline on my dedication to my husband. Let me love and support him in his career for as long as he feels it is right for him, our community, and our family.

8. Police Hate I

Psalm 86:15

But you, O Lord, are a God merciful and gracious, slow to anger and abounding in steadfast love and faithfulness.

The Dorner Case

I was typing away an article in my one-bedroom Honolulu faculty apartment, with my patio open to the view of greenery and a glimpse of Waikiki on a clear day, when I got a call from my then fiancé, Rick, on his day off. He said, "There's a guy shooting cops. I gotta go in today. I just wanted to let you know, but I gotta go. I love you." As quick as he called, he hung up.

He was in a rush. He was always in a rush to save the world. I smiled at myself at that thought. I was typically calm and did not worry about him. I did not have a TV to turn on the news, so I googled "guy shooting cops Los Angeles." I learned that there was a manhunt for a retired Los Angeles city officer and veteran with the last name Dorner who had shot two family members of a Los Angeles officer and had a public manifesto to commit other killings. While I was processing what I was reading and that Rick was on his way to work to help find Dorner, I read the comments of the article:

"F*ck the police"
"Good job, Dorner"
"Kill them all"

It was the first time I had seen the hate for police that Rick had warned me about. I was shocked at how people spoke about police. I did not want to bother Rick at work, so I sat there, feeling alone. I did not know who I could even talk to about all the feelings I was having. I thought about Rick's mom. She did not talk much about what happened to Rick's dad, so I did not contact her. Instead, I called my sister, who did not focus on it too much. She talked about herself- some drama at work, and then we hung up. I texted Rick wishing he were okay, and told him to stay safe. I kept myself busy by continuing to write my article.

Over the next few days, Rick worked a ton of overtime, not just because of Dorner but because he always worked a lot of overtime. He worked swing shift in the South Central Los Angeles gang unit between around 3pm – 3am. Since I was at my first professor job in Hawaii, we had a 3-hour time difference and opposite schedules. I asked him to call me on his way home from work each night and would leave my phone on the nightstand beside my bed. I would answer half asleep, but at least we would get a chance to talk to each other. I asked him how work went; he usually said, "Okay."

I was feeling needy and emotional with the Dorner shooter out there, so I pushed him that night, "No, please, tell me something that happened at work." He responded, "They just keep killing each other. That is why I do not want to talk about it. It is not fun to talk about." I did not know what to say in response to that. I will not say I stopped pushing him to talk about work from that point, but I did not push him anymore that night. I told him about teaching that day and the research I was doing. We exchanged, "I love you," and hung up.

The next day, I got a text from my sister that there were rumors that Dorner was in Las Vegas, where she lived. She was now worried and called to vent while I listened.

Dorner was found dead nine days later in San Bernardino, California. The rumors of him in Las Vegas were not correct.

Prayer

Jesus, let my husband feel your love and the love you have given so many people who support law enforcement. May we fill our lives with those people who support and love our family the way you love. Allow me to thank my husband for all he does in case I am the only one he hears it from each day.

9. How My Officer Sees Things II

Romans 12:10

Love one another with brotherly affection. Outdo one another in showing honor.

Are You Armed?

Before having kids, if Rick had a few days off, we would go out on the second day off together. The first day off was for recovery. On his first day off, Rick usually ran errands like getting his uniforms dry-cleaned, and then we would just "Netflix and Chill."

On this second day off, we went to Downtown Pasadena. We loved this hat store with all wool hats, so we talked about saving up to get two of them. We walked around the shops and did not even buy anything. We just enjoyed strolling around together. Also, we ate at a restaurant and then started driving home in Rick's blacked-out Audi with no plates. Rick believed that perpetrators could find his information at the DMV if they followed him driving out of the station, so he taped his registration to the front window and did not have license plates on his car.

Man, that Audi drove so smoothly. I drove it once when Rick had a bit too much to drink, and I went 100 mph on the 101 freeway without even feeling or hearing it. It was dangerously smooth.

That day, Rick was driving. We had not had anything to drink. Suddenly, he heard the "whoop" siren from a highway patrol car behind us, so he pulled over. He then wound down his window and waited. The officer slowly approached our car and called out, "Are you armed?" Rick, who had a concealed weapon on his belt holster, responded, "Yes, sir, I'm a Los Angeles city officer." The officer told Rick to put his hands on the wheel, and he did as he was told.

I thought, "How did the officer know to ask if he was armed?"

The officer asked why Rick did not have a license plate, and Rick told them what I told you. The officer nodded and said, "Ok. We are just asking that people have their license plates on their cars. Have a good day." That was it. I felt a mutual understanding between the officer and Rick. Rick always said that highway patrol had it bad because they were alone in their patrol cars while city police usually had partners.

Prayer

Heavenly Father, I am thankful for our law enforcement community. There is a common bond that officers share with one another. That common understanding and respect are needed in today's world. Thank you for every moment my husband feels respect or gratitude from a fellow officer or civilian.

10. The Wedding

1 Corinthians 13: 4-13

Love is patient and kind; love does not envy or boast; it is not arrogant or rude. It does not insist on its own way; it is not irritable or resentful; it does not rejoice at wrongdoing but rejoices with the truth. Love bears all things, believes all things, hopes all things, endures all things.

Love never ends. As for prophecies, they will pass away; as for tongues, they will cease; as for knowledge, it will pass away. For we know in part, and we prophesy in part, but when the perfect comes, the partial will pass away. When I was a child, I spoke like a child, I thought like a child, I reasoned like a child. When I became a man, I gave up childish ways. For now, we see in a mirror dimly but then face to face. Now I know in part; then I shall know fully, even as I have been fully known.

So now faith, hope, and love abide, these three; but the greatest of these is love.

Barefoot on the Sand

The day after we got engaged, I asked Rick, "So, where do you want to get married?" as we drove to North Shore, Oahu, for fun. Rick answered, "I want to get married in a church." My surprised, "Ohh…" response made him explain, "marriage is a religious ceremony." I said, "It is?" I laugh as I write this. I have since been educated on this. Now you know why I prefaced this book with telling you I was raised by hippies. My mom taught me to be a good person just because it was the right thing to do.

Rick wanted a big Catholic wedding in a church. That plan ended after calling several Catholic churches in California as a non-Catholic living in Hawaii. The churches were not too excited about us marrying at their church in high demand, populated Los Angeles where we were not even parishioners. I told Rick, "I always wanted to get married on the beach with no shoes on." I found an American Catholic Priest who would marry us on the beach, and Rick quickly agreed. He even agreed to get married barefoot. That man's feet were always covered in socks, usually black, so I was shocked when he agreed to a barefoot wedding.

We found a big beach house on the shore of Oceanside, California, within driving distance to most of our family and friends in Los Angeles and Las Vegas. Our guest list had to be small, under 50 guests, to get married on the sand.

My bridesmaids, including childhood friends, my sister, Rick's sister, my mom, and aunts surrounded me on the wedding day. Rick was with his mom, dad and groomsmen; three out of five were fellow police officers. My girls brought me Starbucks all morning while Rick and his men drank. I am not sure why we thought giving his groomsmen a bottle of moonshine would be a good idea. I was mortified.

Just kidding. Rick was a total gentleman during the ceremony. My mom walked me down the aisle. Rick grabbed my arm and held onto my arm while the priest did mass, and we said our personalized vows. If you read between the lines he spoke, you would hear Rick refer to me putting his gun in my purse on occasion and how I told him I would run away with him to Mexico if anything crazy went down because "she loves Mexican food."

As a child of parents whose metal bat under their bed was their home protection, never did I think that a gun would be referenced in my husband's wedding vows. But now here I am, still accidentally hitting the gun on Rick's hip when I go to touch his back.

Prayer

Heavenly Father, give me patience when I do not feel patience for the many demands of overtime, court, and odd schedules in my husband's career. I pray that my husband gives me grace as I find my role as a police wife. If I feel resentful, I pray that you give me the tools I need to overcome that feeling.

11. Newlyweds

Ecclesiastes 4:9-12

Two are better than one because they have a good reward for their toil. For if they fall, one will lift his fellow. But woe to him who is alone when he falls and has not another to lift him up!

Again, if two lie together, they keep warm, but how can one keep warm alone? And though a man might prevail against one who is alone, two will withstand him—a threefold cord is not quickly broken.

The Honey Do List

I was so excited to spend the summer with Rick as newlyweds. Sure, summers are the busiest season for police officers in Los Angeles. Rick says people get out of their hot homes and get into trouble whenever it heats up. But I had plans for when he was at work. I would sleep in most days and then work on my research from our new apartment Rick surprised me with while he was at work. Then, we would hang out on his days off.

Little did I know that being a newlywed is difficult. There is quite a bit of negotiating. Rick began leaving me "honey-do" lists while he was at work. He asked me to take in his dry cleaning, get the mail at the PO Box, etc.

We had a PO Box because Rick told me criminals could get our address from the DMV. So he told me to use the PO Box address even at the DMV to get my driver's license.

At this time in our newlywed lives, Rick left working in South Central gangs, where he had been for several years. The overtime demanded of him and unstable schedule consumed him. He chose to leave to work in downtown Los Angeles in a different specialized unit with less overtime. This is just one sacrifice Rick made for me over our years of marriage.

One day, Rick gently mentioned that many of his co-worker's wives made them lunches.

I had yet to define myself as a wife. I was still adjusting to life as a partnership.

But I began to make Rick lunches.

Then, he gently said, "You know, it would be nice if you made me breakfast." During that time, Rick worked a very early shift when he would leave at 4:30am. I was like, "Umm.. no, that's kind of early." I had plans of sleeping in that summer, remember?

Rick's mom, Zandra, texted me one day, "OMW." I thought it was a butt text. Later that day, I got a text from Rick that read, "My mom's on her way to visit. She's in Victorville now." Rick was scheduled to work the next few days. Luckily, his mom and I got along great. We went to the beach, and one day, we went out to breakfast.

Over breakfast, I told Zandra, "Rick wants me to wake up early and make him breakfast every morning."

She responded, "Well, aren't you? I cooked my family three hot meals each day."

Raised traditionally in Mexico, Rick's mom was taught homemaking was her responsibility. Although she worked full-time throughout Rick's childhood, she took responsibility for homemaking just as seriously as her day job.

Zandra woke me up, and I became a better wife that day.

Prayer

Lord, I pray today to be a good partner to my spouse. I pray to rid myself of selfishness. I want to be open to the gifts of balance in giving and self-care without selfishness. May I take care of my husband because we are partners in this life. What is good for him is good for me and serves you, Lord.

12. Finances

Matthew 6:21

For where your treasure is, there your heart will be also.

Mini Cooper

I often referred to my husband as a vampire. Not only because he is often awake at night but also because he lived many different lives before I met him at age 21. When Rick was young, he was a car mechanic. As a young adult, he received two associate's degrees in aeronautic engineering and fixed jets. He also helped build The Palms hotel in Las Vegas as a construction worker while he was an undergrad.

If anything was wrong with our cars, Rick always took care of them. Because of his busy schedule, he often took them to a trusted mechanic to get them fixed. At least Rick could diagnose the issue and knew how much it should cost to fix it, unlike clueless me.

The Mini Cooper I was driving needed maintenance, so Rick took it to a mechanic. It needed a lot of work due to the miles I put on it driving back and forth from Las Vegas to Los Angeles for work. Later, Rick called to tell me that it would cost thousands of dollars in repairs. I asked, "Did you already tell them to make the repairs?" To which he answered, "Yes." I was disappointed because I thought we should have considered trading the car for a new one since it had so many miles on it. I was upset that he did not talk to me about this before telling them to make the repairs, but the deed was done.

While every marriage handles finances differently, financial decisions and issues greatly stress marriages. We combined our finances and used a shared bank account. We considered all of our finances to be "ours."

After I calmed down, we talked about financial decisions we would make together. We set a maximum amount that we would spend without discussing it with each other, and if we needed to spend more than that amount, then we needed to consult each other before spending money. That "rule" we made continued with us in our marriage and helped us both feel that we were a part of the "bigger" financial decisions and prevented potential tension or arguments.

Prayer

Heavenly Father, empower us to communicate respectfully about money matters. Remind my husband and me that we are financial partners. Our financial decisions impact one another no matter who earns money through paid work or manages the family's finances. Let us both see that we contribute to the marriage and have a right to financial decision-making. Allow our financial decisions to bring us together with united goals to benefit the family.

13. Faithfulness

Matthew 19:4-6

'Haven't you read,' he replied, 'that at the beginning the Creator 'made them male and female,' and said, 'For this reason, a man will leave his father and mother and be united to his wife, and the two will become one flesh?' So they are no longer two, but one flesh. Therefore what God has joined together, let no one separate.'

A Woman Visited Rick at Work

I interviewed at many conferences while trying to get a job in Los Angeles. Since Rick was local, he came too. One university invited us to a cocktail reception. Something you should know about my career is that it is female dominant. Straight, handsome, muscular men around the office or at conferences are rare. Let me tell you, the ladies at the cocktail reception were all over Rick! I was hoping they would get to know me better, but all they wanted to do was chat with a "cop from our city."

I did not mind. In fact, I joked that Rick should flirt with them to get me the job. I am confident in Rick and my relationship. Despite the long distance, I never worried about cheating. I always felt like we were the kind of people who would not be together if we did not want to be together rather than cheat; it was in our bones.

At the reception, Rick connected with a social worker who worked for a nonprofit that helped human trafficking victims. They exchanged business cards and stayed in touch to help victims together.

Months later, Rick casually tells me that this woman he met at the conference came to his office *on her day off* to chat about a case. My ears perked up. I started interrogating him, "Why did she come by on her day off to discuss work? Why did you not tell me earlier?" I realized that I did get jealous even though I trusted him. He had reasonable explanations for all of it, but I asked him to tell me sooner if they did have a meeting next time. He agreed and did so from then on.

Prayer

I pray for faithfulness in our marriage. I pray that
we remember each day that we joined together in
Your light, God. A marriage is worth protecting.
We must only look to each other for intimate
love and companionship. I pray that even in the
longest months and years when we are so busy
and unable to connect, we are reminded that our
marriage is for a lifetime. We know our marriage
will have years when we feel very connected and
others, especially those early years with young
children, that we might feel less connected
intimately. We will remain faithful during these
times. Bless us with patience as we wait for the
years when we can connect more if we are in that
less connected time.

Heavenly Father, I also ask that you give us a
voice when we need to express something that
makes us uncomfortable. If there is a person in
our spouses' life that we feel is inappropriate, let
us communicate with each other and advocate
for the protection and prioritization of our
marriage and family.

14. Always on Duty

1 Peter 5:7

Casting all your anxieties on him because he cares for you

Japan Visit

The summer after we got married, I had the opportunity to teach in an exchange program for an Okinawan. We traveled to mainland Japan first and ended with a week in Okinawa for my lecture. In mainland Japan, we started in Tokyo, followed by Kyoto, and ended in Osaka.

We biked across a red bridge overlooking a river in Kyoto. We also passed young people in traditional Japanese kimonos, which we did not see much of in Tokyo. I remember wearing one once when I was a kid for a performance in Hawaii. I was sweating as it was high humidity and 80 degrees. Unfortunately, I began to get a rash on my leg. We searched for a pharmacy. Not speaking the language, I was unsure how we could get help. Rick was a natural at exploring new places, and the Japanese people were also so kind in each city we visited. They went out of their way to communicate with us, using their phones to translate. I was forever grateful.

We slowly rode down an alleyway. There was what looked to be a garage open to the alleyway; we could see chairs of men sitting, waiting for something inside. We caught a glimpse of young, barely dressed women inside as well. Rick told me that it was most likely adult dancing or prostitution. Without him there, I would not have thought that.

That night in Kyoto, we were resting in our hotel room. Rick checked his email and was surprised to find an email from a human trafficking victim he thought had returned to prostitution. She came to him after he caught her prostituting to retrieve a cell phone that the police department took into custody. After fidgeting a bit and looking over her shoulder, Rick asked her what was wrong. She told him that her pimp, who trafficked her across state lines, was holding her young daughter captive. Concerned, Rick texted me that he would be home late. That night, he recruited other officers to find her daughter. Luckily, he eventually found the daughter in the middle of the night under the care of an older woman paid by the pimp. They placed her in a car seat in the patrol car and took her back to the station, where the young girl was placed in the custody of child welfare. Rick then informed the trafficking victim that her child had to be with child welfare but that she could be with her daughter again if she found safety herself.

Rick also connected the trafficking victim with a social worker who provided peer support for human trafficking, who he met at the social work conference with me. He further arrested the pimp, but he was released before charges were made. Without a victim, there is no crime, and the trafficking victim did not want to face him in court. Rick lost touch with the victim; over time, he thought she went back to the pimp until he received the email. Her email chronologically outlined what happened after they lost touch. She had returned to the pimp for some time. She sent photos of her lowest moment with bruises covering her face. Those photos were followed by pictures of her happy with her daughter, and she thanked Rick for helping her. She told him that since she was beaten badly, she got the help she needed and could get her daughter back and move back to the state she came from. Rick hardly ever hears "thank you." I know it meant the world to him.

After visiting Osaka, we traveled to Okinawa by plane. Rick always liked to sit on the plane until most people got off before he deboarded the plane. Whenever we did this in the U.S., I found that we had to sit there for what seemed like *forever*. Japanese people were so much more efficient than Americans. They had their bags ready and each row of seats deboarded so quickly, one after another. My lack of patience appreciated it. It took me time to realize that Rick's desire to wait allowed him to remain calm and deboard in a less crowded environment.

We were picked up at the airport by our translator, a 93-year-old Okinawan man who referred to himself as "young." He had a paper that said "Linton," which made my day. He informed us that we would have dinner with a Professor who would host my trip. After getting settled in the hotel, an Okinawan social work student picked us up in his car with another student as a passenger. They had Jay-Z playing on the radio. Rick loves Jay-Z. One of the students was trilingual in Japanese, Okinawan, and English. The other did not speak English, but they rapped to the Jay-Z song much better than I ever could. The students immediately liked Rick and invited him to the next day's lecture. We originally thought Rick would just relax in the hotel while I lectured, but our students had other plans.

The next day, we met at a classroom on campus. Students brought me and Rick coffee. Rick, unlike most cops, was not fond of coffee. He was told by a Training Officer, "Don't be one of those cops stopping at Starbucks," suggesting that those officers were lazy. It took Rick 15 years on the job before he began getting Starbucks occasionally. I, on the other hand, am obsessed with their drinks. I had never had an American student bring me coffee, even though I had been teaching as a university instructor for several years.

The Okinawan social work students were fascinated by Rick's work as a Los Angeles city police officer. They said that because of movies they had seen about Los Angeles, "I would be afraid to visit.". On the last day of class, I asked Rick if he would present on his work in the gang unit in South Central, and he showed photos of gang members and tattoos. One of the photos was of a young boy. Rick said he talked to him one day and then learned that he had been shot dead the next day. I knew Rick had said that the gang members kept shooting each other, but it was much different to see a photo. Rick told this story with an emotionless tone, and I felt bad that he had to relive that memory.

Prayer

Heavenly Father, I pray for peace for my husband. I pray he can get away from it all and not worry about crime, victims, or perpetrators. I pray that he can lose himself in a different place of peace and calm. I will ask my husband to take his vacation time when he can so we can enjoy life together as a family.

I wish for our home to be an escape from it all. While our home may not be perfectly peaceful, I will ensure that it is an overall happy place for our family and a rightful escape for my husband to recover from his work.

15. How My Officer Sees Things III

Ecclesiastes 4:12:

Though one may be overpowered, two can defend themselves. A cord of three strands is not quickly broken.

Maintenance Guy

Rick surprised me with our own one-bedroom apartment when I arrived for the summer after working in Hawaii for the academic year. It was modern, was within walking distance to a little grocery store I loved and had a pool and gym. He had already furnished it! I was excited. It was the first summer of our marriage, and there were a lot of new things. We were figuring each other out, negotiating finances, and dividing household responsibilities. These are normal things that each married couple goes through.

Being married to a police officer posed different experiences, such as the simple visit of an electrician to our apartment as the impetus for an argument.

I was home alone when someone knocked on the door. It was a man that worked for the apartment complex, and he said he needed to fix something. He said he needed to see an electrical unit in the bedroom closet, so I let him in, not thinking anything of it. After he was done, he left.

When Rick was home the next day, I told him I let the electrician into the closet, and he immediately got upset. "You let him into our closet? There are guns in there." I got defensive and said, "How was I supposed to know?" Rick said, "How have you not seen them? He could come back for them." I remained defensive and told Rick, "You cannot expect me to see things the way you do. My mind just does not go there." At the time, I thought Rick was overreacting, and dare I say, I thought he was being paranoid.

Literally, eight years later, I asked Rick what had happened at his shift the previous night, and he said he got to arrest a robber. The robber had been pretending to be a maintenance worker for an apartment complex to get people to open their apartment doors; he would rob them and then leave. Someone called the cops to tell them he was currently at the apartment doing just that.

Rick said he was solo to the apartment complex and recruited the department helicopter to fly over to see if they could spot the robber. With the help of the helicopter, Rick caught the robber on foot outside one of the apartments. When Rick told me this, I thought back to that first summer of our marriage and realized how wrong I was for being so defensive.

Prayer

Jesus, I pray to you for patience and understanding- even for blind acceptance in my early years of marriage when I am still learning to understand. Sometimes I do not fully understand what my spouse is going through or why he may need certain things done a certain way. He may not be able to explain with words why he needs things this way. I pray for patience anyway.

I pray for empathy. As I learn the reasons behind my spouse's actions, I pray that I place myself in his boots to understand where he is coming from.

16. Police Hate II

Isaiah 54:17

No weapon formed against you shall prosper, and every tongue which rises against you in judgement you shall condemn. This is the heritage of the servants of the Lord, and their righteousness is from Me, says the Lord.

"I Work for the City"

Rick's car had over 100,000 miles on it, and something major broke in it. Rick always had a plan; he had been scoping out cars for a while. He looked online and saw a good deal on a gently used BMW, so we went together to the dealership. On the way there, Rick said, "If he asks me what I do for work, I'm going to tell him that I work for the city." I said, "Why?" To which he answered, "Look, I just don't want to deal with it today." I continued to bother Rick, asking him why he would not be proud of being a police officer. I was on a rant about it, and I had not fully opened my eyes to the hate and Rick's lack of energy on his days off to deal with it. Rick just looked at me, exhausted.

We live in a location with a large anti-police community. Rick did not want to deal with any tension about being a law enforcement officer from a car salesman, but he ended up dealing with tension from me.

Prayer

Lord, grant me the understanding of my husband's experience of hate towards his profession. Give me the gift of empathy and listening. Let me see that sometimes questioning my husband's actions can be hurtful. Give me the gift of patience as I sometimes need to wait to truly understand his needs.

17. Injured on Duty II

John 15:12-13

This is my commandment that you love one another as I have loved you. Greater love has no one than this that someone lay down his life for his friends.

The Search Warrant

We rarely meet up with Rick's friends. He is selective in who he considers to be a friend. His list of people he would refer to as "friends" may not be more than you can count on one hand.

Rick invited his best friend, who I know as Res, and his girlfriend to see a movie with us. Rick sat next to his bestie, and we, the girlfriends, sat on the edges. We always joked that we were the third wheel on Rick and his best friend's date with each other. Rick and Res met in the Police Academy. Res was a combat veteran who did multiple tours in Iraq and Afghanistan. Rick, on the other hand, had always wanted to join the military. But his family stopped him from joining when he was younger, and I stopped him when we were engaged. I already thought that he sacrificed enough in police work. Rick and Res were partners for a bit, but it quickly came to a halt when they got a complaint. They never partnered up again though they worked for the same unit for years in South Los Angeles. They remained good friends, nonetheless.

We were all into the movie when I saw Rick and Res whisper sweet nothings into each other's ears. Rick proceeded to look back at the screen. Then, Res whispered something else to him. Again, Rick continued watching the movie. So, I bugged Rick and asked him, "Is everything okay?" He told me, "A co-worker in 77th gangs got shot in the head looking up in the attic looking for a suspect while serving a search warrant." I responded, "Oh my gosh, let's see if we can help him or his family."

I immediately thought of what I could bring his family. My "cure" for anything is always bringing the family food; it is the Hawaiian in me.

Unbeknownst to me, Rick and Res continued to watch the rest of the movie. We all used the restroom after the movie. No one else said another word about their co-worker. We hugged Res and his girlfriend goodbye.

I brought it up in the car with Rick, "Can we take your co-worker some food or something?" Rick answered, "He is recovering right now. He's still in the hospital, and the investigation's underway."

I later learned that they "investigate" an officer-involved shooting by not allowing officers involved to communicate with anyone else for 24 hours. They want to interview each person first. Rick told me he would text me before they took away his phone if he were in that circumstance. He had been involved in one case where that occurred, but we were on a break from our relationship at the time.

If it were up to Rick, we would not have said another word about the shooting. I was new at being his wife, so I poked and prodded my way into discussing it. I said, "How are you feeling about this?" He replied, "I wish I had been there." Do not judge me with this one, but I said, "That's selfish. I want you to be here and safe." Yep, I called the *selfless* man sitting next to me *selfish* for wanting to be there for his friend, his coworker. I was the selfish one. It took Rick and me a decade to finally settle down with each other. I did not want anything to happen to him.

We never did take food to Rick's coworker. I did not approach the situation the right way. I judged Rick instead of supporting him and meeting him where he was with his emotions. I judged him for something I could not possibly understand. Thankfully, his coworker returned to work after surgeries. Rick told me that the officer should return to the streets to show the community they did not get to the officer. This "showing face" may only be temporary as, of course, the officer has been affected.

Prayer

Heavenly Father, thank you for a life partner, a selfless husband who is a good friend to those around him. I am thankful for spending my life with a protector. He will protect our family. I know my husband is also a protector of his coworkers and community. I must reach deep inside for my selflessness and empower my husband to be the protector that he needs to be to serve you, God. May I remind me that my husband's quality as a protector is a gift not just to me but to the world.

18. How My Officer Sees Things IV

Proverbs 2: 6-15

For the Lord gives wisdom; from his mouth come knowledge and understanding; he stores up sound wisdom for the upright; he is a shield to those who walk in integrity, guarding the paths of justice and watching over the way of his saints. Then you will understand righteousness and justice, and equity, every good path; for wisdom will come into your heart, and knowledge will be pleasant to your soul..."

In the Car Wash, Yeah

Prior to having kids, we kept our cars lookin' good. You know those days when your car is not covered in crumbs and sticky stuff with random toys and books everywhere? Yeah, those were the days.

Rick and I were having a peaceful day just sipping some Slurpees and running his car through a self-serve, drive-through car wash together. After we drove through the car wash, three adult men were there to dry off the car. I said, "That's kind of weird that they are here to dry off the car. Normally workers like that are just at the car washes where they clean the inside too."

He said, "If it does not look right, then it isn't. It's probably a mafia front."

Prayer

I pray to you, Lord, to give my husband your wisdom to shield him while he is working. Allow him to gain knowledge about the world around him as he listens to your voice and messages.

19. Motherhood I- Making a Baby

Psalm 113:9

He settles the childless woman in her home as a happy mother of children. Praise the Lord.

Making a Maverick

When Rick and I decided we wanted to get pregnant, I went off birth control pills. We would try to make a baby while I was home in the summer. We would be juggling a long-distance relationship, police schedule over time, and court days once Fall came. I just did not know how we would have time to make a baby after Fall came. Ideally, we would have a baby in early summer since I was off for the summer from teaching.

I read every article I could about successfully getting pregnant and how birth control can affect pregnancy. The first month, we had sex as often as possible, but I did not track anything. The second month, I tried to track when I thought I was ovulating, but of course, those ended up being long workdays for Rick, and who knows if

I was really ovulating then! In the third month, I decided to get ovulation strips that let you know when you start ovulating. I was so excited to know this information. We were able to have sex on one of the days I ovulated…and a miracle happened; we made a baby.

Prayer

Heavenly Father, I pray to you for the gift of a baby. While I cannot even fathom understanding the miracle of conception, I pray to you to let you know that I am ready to be a mom. I am ready to protect and make sacrifices for my child. I will embrace motherhood's journey and joy, including the challenges and moments of pure happiness.

I am ready for the unique hurdles that being a police wife has in store for me as I enter motherhood. I am preparing myself for long stretches of days of solo parenting. I will begin to build my village of women to support me in motherhood for those solo parenting days. I will prioritize our family time when my husband is home so he can spend time with our children. Lord, remind me to ask for help when I need it.

20. Wives Make Sacrifices Too

Romans 12: 6-8

In his grace, God has given us different gifts for doing certain things well. So if God has given you the ability to prophesy, speak out with as much faith as God has given you. If your gift is serving others, serve them well.

Couples' Natural Birth Class

While pregnant, I was working two jobs. I had moved to a Las Vegas university as a professor after two years in Hawaii. I could not get a job in Los Angeles, but Vegas got me closer to Rick. I also worked on Fridays at a California university to try to get my "in" to the California university system. While pregnant, I drove back and forth from Vegas to Los Angeles almost weekly to work and then saw Rick on the weekends if he was off work.

As I drove back from Las Vegas to Los Angeles on Thursdays, I stopped at a prenatal yoga class in Westlake, California. Stretching after the long drive felt so good, and I loved the teacher. She promoted non-medicated birth, which I was determined to have. She also held a couple's course on non-medicated birth strategies that many other moms signed up for. I tried to sign up for it, but I told her that my husband worked evenings often and would not be able to make it to each class. I then asked if it was important for him to be there in each class.

She said, "Yes. The fathers need to be present in each class. They need to learn to support you in these methods of childbirth."

I was bummed to hear that and felt her judgment like Rick was not supportive if he would not be able to make it. I got defensive but still loved her prenatal yoga classes.

I learned that day that our lives were different as a police family. The world would not accommodate us. We needed to find places, spaces, and communities where we felt supported.

Prayer

Lord, I pray for strength and confidence in my role as a police wife. I pray that you surround me with a community that supports and lifts me up and accepts my unique role as a police wife. This life has demands that other lives do not. I am ready to fulfill the role you have created for me.

21. Communication

1 Thessalonians 5:11

Therefore encourage one another and build one another up, just as you are doing.

We are His Happy Place

I often met up with a fellow police wife who was pregnant at the same time as me at prenatal yoga. Her husband was Rick's current partner at the time. She would regularly come to class and say, "Did you hear what happened last night?" I would say, "No." She would continue with stories of our husband's interactions with perpetrators, arrests they made, and other stories I did not know. When I asked Rick about work, he would say it went well and not much more. Sometimes this bothered me. When I brought it up to Rick, he said, "I do not like talking about work. It is not fun for me. I just want to focus on you and our son." We were his happy place; this finally started to sink in.

Prayer

Jesus, let me remember that somedays, I need not pry to ask questions but just be. Somedays, my husband just needs my presence. Even if he will not speak to me about work, I will be physically and mentally present to enjoy time with him. We will enjoy being together, which will help wash away the "demons" he experiences at work. If he ever wants to speak, I pray I am ready to listen without judgment.

22. Bullets Found Where?

Ecclesiastes 3:4

A time to weep, and a time to laugh; a time to mourn, and a time to dance

Bullet in my Purse

We were traveling home from a conference I presented my research at in New Mexico while pregnant. I was flying back to Las Vegas for work, and Rick was headed home to Los Angeles. We were going through a tiny airport security check-in when I placed my purse on the conveyor belt to go through the scanner. Gently, I was waiting to walk through the body scanner when they called me to return to a security person before I could proceed. The security person had my purse. She said, "So you have anything to tell me?" I said, "No," thinking they finally found the pepper spray on my keychain I had flown with many times, and airport security never said anything about it. But, no, it was not my pepper spray.

She pulled a bullet out of my purse.

Remember when I told you my family had a bat in my home for security when I was growing up? Even though I married a man who carried a gun most of the time, I was clueless about guns; that was *not* my bullet.

I said, "I don't know how that got in there." She said, "We are going to need to dispose of it." I said, "Okay." She then asked me to throw it away, which I did. Then, she let me go through security again. Rick, on the other hand, already got through. He was sitting waiting for me. I told him, "They found a bullet in my purse!"

He smiled, "Yeah. I put it in there so you would think of me."

Prayer

Lord, thank you for blessing me with a husband that makes me laugh. Thank you for a husband who keeps me on my toes. While I may never fully understand his love language or jokes, give me laughter. Let me laugh at the idiosyncrasy of each bullet in the washing machine or… purse… or wherever I may find them. Let us laugh

heelsandholster: a police wife devotional

together in the good and bad, for laughter is healing.

23. Motherhood II- Preparing for Childbirth

1 Peters 5:7

Casting all your anxieties on him because he cares for you.

Preparing for Baby Maverick

I signed Rick and I up for a childbirth class at the hospital. Rick made almost every class, but no joke, I would catch him with his eyes closed. Poor guy was always tired and a bit off due to mostly working night shifts. By now, he had switched to working a new gang unit in Northridge on the night shift.

Rick really liked the class on pain management during childbirth. He supported my choice to want a nonmedicated birth, but he did not want me in pain. I felt confident going into labor with Rick by my side. He was always calm, cool, and collected. He would be my rock.

I *was* nervous that Rick would not be there during childbirth. When he was at work, he was very busy in the gang unit. We rarely spoke on the phone when he was working. Most of the time, we just texted so he could respond when he had a moment. I looked up Rick's station phone number just in case I needed to call there to get ahold of him. I even tried calling it once to ensure I got ahold of a person. Little did I know that it is usually a cop stuck at the station answering that line. Also, people call the station phone number to ask for law enforcement advice. Rick's station even got called about a turtle crawling down the road in Los Angeles once! You learn new things every day as a police wife!

Prayer

Heavenly Father, I know that you will calm my anxiety if I call you. I pray that you remind me that you will take all my anxieties if I leave them with you.

24. Motherhood III-Childbirth I

Psalm 139:13

I praise you because I am fearfully and wonderfully made; your works are wonderful. I know that full well.

Welcoming Baby Maverick

I felt contractions around midnight on May 21st, about a week before Maverick's expected due date. The contractions woke me up; back then, I slept like a rock, and nothing woke me up. I moved from my bed to the couch, put a show on, and started tracking how often the contractions came. They started speeding up around 2am. Immediately, I texted Rick, "Come home on time tonight. I think it is time. I'm having contractions." He instantly responded that he was on his way. Rick typically got off work around 2am without overtime, so Maverick's timing was perfect. When Rick got home, I was uncomfortable, curled up in a ball on the couch. I then called the doctor, who told me to come to the hospital. Rick grabbed a bag I packed, and off we went.

Once we got to the hospital, the nurse informed me that my contractions had slowed. She said, "Try to get some sleep," and left the room. Rick laid beside me on a couch, exhausted from the 12-hour shift. I, at least, had some sleep before coming to the hospital. I turned on a show on the TV in the hospital room. As I relaxed, the contractions began to return.

The nurse checked on me, and I told her I was uncomfortable. She told me to try taking a shower and going for a walk around the hospital. I was only dilated 4 cm.

I did as I was told, starting with the shower. *Oh my gosh, I should have stayed in there.* It felt so good to have the water run on my back. No one ever tells you that your back hurts during labor! I felt insecure about using up all the water, so I decided to go for a walk.

After getting out of the shower, I saw Rick asleep on the couch, and I walked the hospital halls.

That was when I saw an angel.

She was pushing her newborn baby in a bassinet. She asked me, "Are you in labor? How are you doing?" I told her, "Yes. Not well. I'm really uncomfortable." She asked, "Did you get the epidural?" I answered, "No. I really want to have an all-natural birth." She said, "I did not get one for my first baby. I got one this time around, and I was in labor, laughing with my husband. It was so nice!" She kept walking; the conversation happened in passing.

After having Maverick and realizing that I was placed in a room in an entirely different Mother-Baby hospital unit after labor, I found it odd that she was in the Labor and Delivery unit walking with her newborn. I call her an angel because of this.

When I got back to the room, my doctor was there. So I told her and my nurse that I was in a lot of pain, and she suggested I get an epidural. Rick was awake then too. I said, "Okay, I'll get it," mostly because the angel made me envision laughing with Rick instead of waddling back and forth in pain like I was.

The angel was right. After getting the epidural, the nurse told me, "You just had a contraction." I laughed because I felt none of it.

Maverick was born after 30 minutes of pushing. We did not know his sex until he was born. Our doctor held him up and said, "It's a boy!" She did not know his sex either. He was perfect; I held him on my chest, and... he peed on me not once but twice. Welcome to motherhood!

Prayer

Lord, Earth is as it is in Heaven with our baby. Thank you for this gift of life with ten little fingers and ten little toes. I am forever grateful for our baby. Grant my body the strength to meet our baby's needs in breastfeeding or bottle feeding if that is best for us. Bless me to raise my baby in a happy home in partnership with my husband. Bless the warmth of our bodies to bring our baby peace. I pray for your invisible protection over our vulnerable baby. Send us the knowledge to know what to do when our baby cries, even if it is just to hold him or her. Give us the skills to swaddle him or her so our baby feels comfortable and sleeps well. Grant us love and patience to pour over our sweet baby.

25. Hypervigilance I

2 Corinthians 4:18

As we look not to the things that are seen but to the things that are unseen. For the things that are seen are transient, but the things that are unseen are eternal.

Jogging with Maverick

Maverick was tiny, not especially tiny for a baby. He was 6 pounds, 12 ounces, which was average for a US-born baby. But I felt that he was so tiny. I felt like I could break him. I was a nervous wreck of a mom. I had not yet learned how to ask for help, so I was determined to do everything perfectly and on my own. Rick was able to take a month off after we had Maverick, but after that, I was home alone with my little angel while Rick worked a lot of overtime in the gang unit.

This was a very difficult time in our marriage. I regularly told Rick, "You're never home." I look back on this and know it was not helpful. I know it was hurtful to Rick when he wanted to be home with us, but he had to work. I was lost in a funk of resentment and loneliness.

I did resistance training for exercise even up until the day I went into labor with Maverick. I knew working out made me happy, so I started some at-home workouts when Maverick was an infant while he napped.

The prenatal yoga I went to also offered postpartum moms to come after they had their babies for postnatal yoga. When Maverick was just 7 weeks old, I took him back to class with me. In the class, I met other local moms that saved me from postpartum depression and loneliness in those early mom days in a new city.

As soon as I could get approval to go jogging with Maverick, I jumped at it. We had even gotten a jogging stroller before we had Maverick.

One day, I casually told Rick, "I'm going to start jogging with Maverick." I did not think much of telling him except just to tell him what was on my mind. He supported me and cheered me on whenever I worked out.

A couple of days later, Rick nonchalantly
he checked out a good running path for r
the neighborhood. He added that I should run
down a specific street in one direction and then
back. He then said I should not run in the other
direction on that road, prompting me to ask,
"Why?"

He explained that there was an apartment
complex and a rough neighborhood in the other
direction, and he did not want me to run over
there. He needed to know that Maverick and I
were safe when he was at work; that seemed
reasonable. I agreed to his planned running path.

Postpartum Stroller Run Prayer

Heavenly Father, bless me to see the things that
are unseen or invisible. While it could take years
for me to wrap my head around where my
husband is coming from, empower me to
empathize with him the best I can without
judgment. Allow me to learn to read through the
lines of his words and let his body language or
tone of voice speak for him. I will give my
husband grace and honor his wishes for specific
accommodations that I may not understand now
or ever.

26. Motherhood IV- The Baby Stage

Matthew 11:28-30

Come to Me, all who are weary and heavy-laden, and I will give you rest. Take My yoke upon you and learn from Me, for I am gentle and humble in heart, and you will find rest for your souls. For My yoke is easy and My burden is light.

Maverick's First Year

Do not try this at home.

Rick and I had this grand idea that we would juggle opposite work schedules and would not need daycare help for Maverick. Rick would work the swing shift late afternoons through early-morning. He would then be home in time for me to teach in the mornings, and I would be home in time for him to go to work.

And we would never sleep again.

In all seriousness, I am not quite sure what we were thinking with this idea, but we did it for Maverick's first year of life. We loved Maverick so much and feared other people caring for him outside of the family. Most of our family did not live close, though, so it was difficult for them to help. The exception was my aunt, who I could not thank enough for helping us in multiple binds when Rick would have overtime, and I would text her last minute to watch Maverick while I went to teach my class. We are forever grateful for her.

After that crazy first year, we were both sleep-deprived, and Maverick was older, so we found a home daycare we loved for him. We were referred to her by a mom friend, Dana, whom I met in my prenatal yoga class. Dana had started her son at the same home daycare just a few months prior. The daycare teacher was so loving and organized the children's day with a bit of structure but enough time to play. Her values were the same as ours. She cared for our children for three years.

Prayer

Lord, bless me with the humility to ask for help when needed. Our family has unique sacrifices as a police family. More burdens are placed on our shoulders than most. May we find a community of people with shared values that we trust to help us in our homes and with our children.

27. Resentment

Romans 12:10

Be devoted to one another in love. Honor one another above yourselves.

Bulletproof

I knew I was resentful of Rick being gone so much for work. My resentment improved once I began making friends and we got daycare. But I remember a specific moment that changed me. Rick's work partner suggested we watch this Christian movie about marriage. We were not quite sure how the movie would be, but we tried it one night together.

The movie "Fireproof" showed a married couple struggling. The husband consulted God and the Church. He was advised to show his wife love for a certain amount of time before giving up on the marriage. It reminded me of a fake it 'til you make it type of advice. He began telling her that he loved her, gave her gifts, and did things for her to show her that he cared. After some time, she began to feel loved. Then, she began to show her husband love in return.

I heard this message loud and clear. Since then, I stopped doing hurtful things in our marriage, like telling Rick he was never home. I began focusing on all the good things Rick did. I began noticing all the little things he did to care for our family and told him that I was thankful and loved him.

Over time, this changed us. It did not happen overnight, but eventually, I literally did not feel annoyed about his work schedule changing last minute or overtime shifts. I had accepted that his chaotic schedule was a part of *our* lives.

We had taken the practical steps, such as getting daycare for Maverick, to address my needs as a working mom whose husband had an unreliable work schedule.

I still had to do the mindset shift. Once I did that, I started seeing Rick change too. He started initiating vacations. He wanted to take time off with the family. Quality time was my love language, and it made me so happy. I also needed some peaceful alone time or time to run errands. When Rick was home, he would tell me, "Go take a shower. Go grocery shopping. Take your time. Grab a coffee…," to give me some much-needed "me time."

Prayer

Lord, I pray that I have gratitude for all the little and big things my husband does for our family. I will write these down when I need a reminder. I will tell my husband what I am thankful for. I will shower my husband with love without the expectation of immediate return. I will be patient to see how my expression of love and gratitude to my husband will change my mindset and improve our relationship over time.

I will accept that we are a police family and all that comes with this life. I will no longer fight or get frustrated with the chaos and stress of being a police wife. Lord, give me the strength to see this clearly. I will recognize that this life is unique, but *we* make sacrifices as a police family for you, God. I am in this life together as a partner with my husband. I will support him as he supports me.

28. Loneliness

Genesis 3:20

"The man called his wife's name Eve because she was the mother of all living."

My Tribe

After postnatal yoga, a girl in the class told me she was starting an online mom group called Little Bunnies for moms of babies born the same year as Maverick. I immediately joined because I did not know anyone else in this huge city. The moms in the group organized play dates sporadically and holiday-themed parties. We all discussed what it was like with sleepless nights and watching our babies learn new things. Sometimes the play dates were short because babies would get tired, but it got us all out of the house around other adults. Sometimes Rick would be off during one of the play dates, but I would still go to the meetup with my new mom friends even if Rick wanted to join. I knew I needed other people in my life locally besides Rick.

Over time as our babies grew, the mom group split apart, but the relationships I built with a couple of the moms remained.

One mom, Amy, and I are the same age and both working moms. We also had both moved to Los Angeles at the same time with no immediate family around. We would text each other and vent or ask questions about motherhood. We would get together with our boys about once a month. I could text her that Rick was working a lot of weekends a certain month, and we would plan a playdate. She helped me get through some lonely solo weekends.

Rick and I were at a check-up appointment less than two years after having Maverick for my second pregnancy with Leonidas. He was constantly kicking, hitting, and or dancing in my tummy. It was a party in there during my second pregnancy. We saw Amy and her husband entering the OBGYN's office door. Now, I do not bring Rick along when I go for my annual checkup. Amy checked in, and I said, "What are you guys doing here?" She answered that they were expecting their second child too! I am so blessed to share this journey of motherhood with Amy and my other friends.

Prayer

Lord, let me see that in my role as a wife or mom, I am a part of a community. Bless me to be surrounded by other wives and mothers who understand me whether or not they are fellow first responder wives. Bless me with a community of women that let me feel seen, to go to for advice, and lean on when I am feeling down. I will go to these women for advice, a shoulder to cry on, and relate with them during my journey as a police wife and in motherhood.

If I do not have a tribe, I will be brave and seek out my wife and mom tribe by joining church groups, wife and mom groups online, and local classes to meet new friends.

29. Motherhood V- Childbirth II

Isaiah 41:10

Fear not, for I am with you; be not dismayed, for I am your God; I will strengthen you, I will help you, I will uphold you with my righteous right hand.

Welcoming Baby Leonidas

Leonidas' birth was completely different. First, Rick was home the day I went into labor. Earlier that day, Rick and I were giving Maverick a bath. I told him, "I want you to know I'm having contractions." Of course, just like babies do, they come when they are ready. My mom already had a flight the next day to come to Los Angeles to help us, but Leonidas wanted to arrive a week early, just like Maverick. We had a babysitter on backup; I called her calm as a clam. The contractions were not bothering me this time. I was able to put Maverick to bed. I kissed him "good night," rubbed his back, and told him I might not be there when he woke up because, "I think baby brother is coming." Our babysitter came over, we called the doctor, and we went right to the hospital.

While the nurse checked me in, she said, "You have been having contractions the whole time I've been talking to you. You are doing very well." I barely felt them this time, and I was already 7 cm dilated. I decided to get the epidural anyway because it went so well the last time.

Things did not go the same way as in my first labor. I did not know until he was born, but Leonidas was sunny side up, or in the posterior position, in which his head was facing down but facing my abdomen. His skull was against the back of my pelvis.

Long story short, my blood pressure dropped, but Leonidas did not. I had the epidural. I was stuck lying there, unable to do the squat position. The epidural went to my leg, which I could not move for hours after Leonidas was born. My mantra, which I did say out loud, was, "Ride it like a wave. Your body was meant for this." Rick played music for me to try to calm me.

With the help of some Pitocin and a "peanut" pillow under my leg, Leonidas eventually dropped. I was so afraid of a c-section, so I ugly-pushed him out. I think I still pretended to look pretty while pushing Maverick out, but with Leonidas, I just did not care about anything else but getting him out.

Leonidas was perfect and strong, just like his name suggests.

The doctor had to sew me up good. It took over two months before my stitches were out and for me to heal.

Prayer

Lord, strengthen me when I am weak. Give me the gift of determination to push through the pain of childbirth. Pain is only temporary. Remind me that my body is made for childbirth. Put me in touch with my body. Allow me to listen to my body and trust that it knows what to do during childbirth. Bless my husband to be strong and give me encouragement during labor.

When our eyes see our baby, let us take a moment to enjoy the peace it brings. Seeing our baby is such a special love. Allow us to reflect on how our love for our baby is as close as we will get to Your love for us. Let our lives be transformed by parenthood as we are now always responsible for our children.

When our baby meets his or her siblings, may they know that they are now responsible for their brother or sister. We protect one another as a family.

30. Concealed Carry

Psalms 144:1

Of David. Blessed be the Lord, my rock, who trains my hands for war and my fingers for battle.

Toddler Music & a Gun

Rick legally carries his gun in a holster on his belt most of the time. His department informs them they are expected to step into any situation on or "off duty" when law enforcement is needed. We live in a politically liberal state with limiting gun laws. Not a lot of people carry concealed weapons.

One day, we attended a trial toddler music class at our local Parks and Recreation for Leonidas. Both our boys had a blast. We were lucky that Rick was with us. He danced around with our boys and had fun too.

I tried to inform the person in charge of the class that I wanted to permanently register via email. But I did not get a response. Instead, I received an awkward phone call from a representative at

Parks and Recreation. She said, "I have not gotten back to you about registering because we had a complaint from a parent in the class that your husband had a gun." I said, "Oh, he's a cop. It's legal for him to carry." She laughed and said, "What a relief. But would it be possible for him not to carry on our property?" I tried explaining to her that he was told to intervene no matter where he was, and since many perpetrators have guns, he needed to carry it with him. She again asked if he could "just not have it with him during class." I politely hung up with her and never returned to that class. We have found other recreation activities for Leonidas where our family is accepted.

At a local jiujitsu class, a woman once asked me, "Is your husband a cop? I saw the gun on his hip." I answered, "Yes, he is." She then said, "That's wonderful. My husband is an officer too. Where does he work?" I was so thankful that she asked, and I felt safe there.

Prayer

Heavenly Father, thank you for giving my husband the gifts of skills and tools to keep him safe while he is enforcing the law. As his wife, I will support him in gaining the skills he needs to fight crime, whether it be tactical or weaponry expertise. For as long as the perpetrators have these skills, I know that my husband needs to know more to make it home to us after each shift. Practically, I will give him time to perfect his skills and build muscle and strength. Politically, I will defend his rights and educate those ignorant about his profession.

31. Prioritizing Our Marriage

1 Timothy 5:8

But if someone doesn't provide for their own family, and especially for a member of their household, they have denied the faith. They are worse than those who have no faith.

My Ohana

When Leonidas was just 10 months old, my mom wanted my sister's family and mine to go to the Big Island in Hawaii. I was nervous about traveling with a 10-month-old and 3-year-old, but I was excited to show Rick where I was from.

It was a beautiful trip as Leonidas was just starting to walk. The water was so warm there, and I remember Maverick swimming from Rick to his grandma in the ocean. Rick brought a knife to crack open coconuts and chopped down bamboo. That man is in his element outdoors. We got to have a special lunch hosted by my half-brother at a 5-star restaurant he managed and then went to a nearby playground.

While we were there, I followed my sister and mom's lead on things to do each day except one day when we did a day trip to the small town I grew up in, Hilo. That day trip was super quick. In Hilo style, it rained on us as well. My grandmother used to always say, "You brought the rain," when we visited her even though it rains almost every day there.

When we got home from this trip to paradise, Rick told me he was upset with me. He had wanted to visit the volcanoes erupting, and I never allowed it to happen. I did not prioritize it. I was not used to prioritizing my small family, my husband's desires on big family trips. It was our first big trip with my sister, mom, Rick, and our boys. I felt awful and still do. I hope to redo a small family trip to Hawaii.

Prayer

Lord, I ask that you give me clarity on my role as wife and mother. It can take time to adjust to a new role in a new family within the context of a larger family unit.

Empower me to stand strong in prioritizing God, my husband, and then our children more than anyone else. Bless my siblings and our parents to understand that our little family must prioritize one another in our new roles as husband and wife. If we have energy or time remaining, then, of course, we will care for the needs of others.

32. Hypervigilance II

Proverbs 12:25

An anxious heart weighs a man down, but a kind word cheers him up.

I Lost Maverick

I was at a park with Maverick, three years old, and Leonidas, about one-year-old, a newly walking, drunken monkey toddler. I was chasing Leonidas around the playground and keeping an eye on Maverick, who usually stayed very close by. Suddenly, I looked up and did not see Maverick. Panic-stricken, I called for him, but he did not respond. I looked inside the playground tunnel and did not see him. Now, my heart was racing. There was another playground about 30 feet from the one we were at. It did have a small space that I could not see, but I assumed he would not go that far away without telling me.

Within 10 seconds, my mind went to, "Oh my God, someone took him."

I started yelling, "Maverick! Maverick!" Another parent asked me what he was wearing. Then, probably within a minute or two, another parent yelled, "He's over here." He was in the small space I could not see from where I was standing at the other playground.

Maverick came walking out of the playground like, "What's wrong, Mom?"

I hugged him and shook my head. Thank God he was okay. I realized I must have looked a little crazy.

From then on, for as long as my children were little, I found playgrounds that were gated in so I could keep a better eye on them and know they were safe. It relieved my anxiety.

Prayer

Lord, I seek you to calm me in recognition that the traumas my husband endures may be passed onto me and manifest as anxieties. Please bless me with resilience and peace regardless of these secondary traumas that may affect me. Give me the skills I need to see the world as my officer sees it through a lens of strength, not anxiety.

33. Motherhood VI- Raising Children of a Police Officer

1 Corinthians 14:40

But all things should be done decently and in order.

Is Daddy Working Today?

As our boys got a bit older and more aware of our family routines, it became a normal part of our solo morning routines for our boys to ask me, "Is daddy working today?"

Rick's schedule, called a DP or Deployment Period, changed every four weeks. He did not have consistent weekly days on or off within those four weeks. It was chaotic. I often joke with Rick that I want the job of the Los Angeles city police scheduler. I think I could figure out a better way to do things. The instability of Rick's work schedule made it difficult for me to keep track of and even harder for me to explain to our young boys.

To solve this dilemma, I asked Rick if he could send me his DP whenever he got it. I put up a whiteboard calendar low enough for our boys to see it. I updated it with icons or drawings to indicate when "daddy was working" so we could look at the calendar together. While we know overtime or court could change things, at least it gave us something. My boys loved to draw on the calendar with me too. The whiteboard calendar has been useful in keeping track of the entire family's schedule, such as school events, sports, my work, etc. I use a Google calendar as well so I have our family schedule with me wherever we go.

Prayer

Lord, bless me with patience to deal with the chaotic police work schedule. Bless me with low expectations, so I will not be let down if my husband's schedule unexpectedly changes. Let us be as organized as possible as a family, so we are prepared for the unexpected. Give me a backup plan for each backup plan. Or let me hand over my anxieties to you and stop trying to control things out of my control.

34. Holidays

Jeremiah 10:3-5

The rituals of the nations are hollow: A tree from the forest is chopped down and shaped by the craftsman's tools. It's overlaid with silver and gold and fastened securely with hammer and nails so it won't fall over. They are no different than a scarecrow in a cucumber patch: they can't speak; they must be carried because they can't walk. Don't be afraid of them because they can't do harm or good.

Christmas

When we did not have children, we easily adjusted for holidays when Rick worked by celebrating together when Rick was off work. After having children, something changed for me. I wanted consistency for our children in daily routines and on holidays. Oftentimes, I was that consistency. I was able to be there with our children each morning before school and after school to establish consistent routines.

Holidays were always special for Rick and me, even if we celebrated them on a different day or time due to his work schedule. Rick loved it when I decorated for the holidays. He even brought his own traditions into our family holiday traditions, such as cutting down a tree each Christmas. He also puts out his own funny Halloween décor each year.

Many people share a tradition that I brought to our little family for Christmas: having breakfast, opening stockings, and opening presents together as a family on Christmas morning. Because I did not grow up in a church-going family, this was our tradition.

During our children's first few years, Rick was working nights with inconsistent days off. Because he worked nights, I figured he could be there for Christmas morning, whether he worked Christmas Eve night or Christmas Day later. I told Rick that it was important to me that we were together on Christmas morning as a family. I even told him that I would still open the stockings and presents with our boys if he were not there. But Rick made it work. Those first few Christmas mornings, Rick, though usually sleep-deprived, was physically present, having breakfast and opening stockings and presents with our boys and me.

I know you are probably reading this and thinking, "Girl, why was this so important to you?" There was something magical to me about Christmas morning as a kid. While I know that Christmas is not about the gifts, it is about Jesus and family. I remembered celebrating with my family, not necessarily the gifts we shared. I wanted my boys to remember spending Christmas with our family too. We sacrifice a lot in this police wife's life. Sometimes it is okay to put your foot down on something meaningful to you.

Prayer

Jesus, while many holiday traditions may need to accommodate my husband's schedule, let there be some traditions that can remain year after year for our family. Some years, life's instability, chaos, or general business distracts us from family time. These traditions bring us back together at specific times each year. They can be the glue when other priorities may want to pull apart. These traditions may need to be rescheduled, but they can still be shared each year.

Remind me that I am the consistency for my family. I create routines and ensure that traditions are prioritized regardless of anything else that may occur.

Thank you for giving us holidays to focus on you, Jesus, our marriage, and our family.

35. Mexican Restaurant

Proverbs 27:15

A quarrelsome wife is like the dripping of a leaky roof in a rainstorm.

Mexican Restaurant

Indeed, I love Mexican food. We drove by this restaurant down the road from our house a million times. As parents of young kids, we do not get out much, but I said to Rick, "Hey, we should go there." He said, "I've been meaning to tell you that it's a little sketchy. It always has a ton of cars outside late at night. I think it's a place where people go to meet women." Confused, I said, "What? No." It's located right next to nice, suburban neighborhoods. He continued, "It's a prostitution ring. We can't go there."

I told him right then and there that our marriage was over. I had the right to Mexican food. I could sacrifice his safety and not seeing him due to overtime and court for his job, but I could not sacrifice Mexican food. That was just too much to ask.

Prayer

Jesus, this is your humble servant, Lord. I want you to know that the end of that last story is a joke. But, in all seriousness, can you please not let any other restaurants be forbidden to me due to criminal activity? Your girl's hungry and lives for Mexican food. Amen.

36. Finding Peace I

Luke 6:48

He is like a man which built a house, and digged deep, and laid the foundation on a rock: and when the flood arose, the stream beat vehemently upon that house, and could not shake it: for it was founded upon a rock.

Shaver Lake

We took a family trip to an area near Yosemite National Forest called Shaver Lake. Rick said he saw there was still snow up there, and we wanted to play in the snow with our boys. As we drove up, we saw snow melting and rivers flowing in between tall, huge dark green forest trees towering over us. As we reached higher into the mountains, the sides of the roads and trees with covered with white snow. I had never seen so much snow! There was literally about 8 feet of snow piled up on the side of the road from the paved road.

We stayed in an Airbnb house with five acres of property. We cooked at the house, explored, played in the snow on the property, went sledding, and made s'mores as we watched a powerful river flowing right outside the house on the property through a huge glass window. It was peaceful. Rick was calm and happy, and so was I.

Prayer

Lord, my husband is our rock. Even as strong as he appears, his strength needs to rebuild. Allow us to renew his strength in the sunshine amongst the trees outdoors. Remind me to make time to camp, climb mountains, swim in the ocean, and explore the outdoors together as a family. While my husband's job is so important, it can devour him. Lord, tell him when he needs a break to rest. Empower him to use his vacation time to recover.

37. Injured on Duty III

Corinthians 4:17

For this light momentary affliction is preparing for us an eternal weight of glory beyond all comparison.

Rick's Back Surgery

Rick had been in a scuffle with a perpetrator years prior. I still do not know the details of the situation, but I know it screwed up his back. The discs that stabilize our backbones and prevent them from rubbing against nerves and one another were gone at the bottom of his back. There were days he would lie down on the ground in pain. He did not say anything, but I could see it.

He got physical therapy, but it did not work. Hence, he needed surgery. He was not even 40 years old.

Rick's mom came into town to help us out with the boys. I dropped them off at school, and then we went to a hospital to drop Rick off for surgery. At first, I was not nervous.

I was sitting there in the almost empty waiting room. I worked a bit on my laptop and kept an eye on the news. During this time, the COVID-19 virus had begun spreading around the world. As I was waiting on Rick to finish the surgery, a national emergency was announced due to the COVID-19 pandemic. While Rick was asleep, our world changed.

The surgery took two hours longer than expected. I did start worrying that something was wrong that last hour. He had more bleeding than expected, but the doctor told me the surgery was successful. He lengthened and stabilized Rick's backbone. Rick's mom thought she would come by to see Rick since our boys were at school, but the doctor would not let her because of COVID-19.

When I walked into the hospital room, Rick was pale. As always, he was calm. I told him about the national emergency and he kind of shrugged. He wanted me to get our boys from school and be with his mom. Because of COVID-19, Rick ended up being the nurses' only patient. They waited on him hand and foot and fed him whenever he wanted. Those nurses would be hard to live up to, so I told them to just keep him there.

Okay, eventually, they kicked him out of the hospital. Rick was home but stuck resting for much longer than we expected. We have a townhome, and he mostly stayed in our upstairs bedroom for about a month. He only came downstairs to our living room for meals after a couple weeks. Our boys hung out with him in the bedroom and watched shows.

During this period, I was in survival mode. My boys' school closed due to COVID-19 for most of that spring semester. The university I worked for transitioned to virtual teaching. I was juggling caring for Rick and my boys and teaching full time. I remember someone telling me that I should focus on the basics when in tough times. Eat right, exercise, and depend on routines that work. That is exactly what I did. I remember folding the laundry right outside the dryer because it was most efficient. I would then put it away right away. I did not stop thinking or complaining; I just got stuff done.

After some time, Rick was ready for physical therapy, but no offices were open. Eventually, he started physical therapy, and things really improved for us. Rick followed therapy with CrossFit, wrestling, and Brazilian Jiujitsu.

Thankfully, he gained a ton of muscle weight and was in the best shape of his life.

With schools and even playgrounds closed in our state, I was so grateful for neighbors with children who broke the "social distancing" rules and let our children play together outside in our neighborhood; this saved us. People are so important.

To this day, Rick tells his friends how much I was there for him during that time.

Prayer

Lord, give us faith that the momentary struggles will be worthwhile in the long run. Injuries are common among law enforcement officers. As a police wife, injuries can be unsettling like other unstable parts of the law enforcement career. Bless me with faith in You to heal my husband from any injuries. Let my husband use any recovery time for physical injuries to rest and recover his mind and emotions. Let hims rebuild stronger.

38. Police Hate III

Isaiah 6:10

Render the hearts of this people insensitive, their ears dull, and their eyes dim, otherwise they might see with their eyes, hear with their ears, understand with their hearts, and return and be healed.

White Silence is Violence

2020 changed me. Black Lives Matter (BLM) protests broke out all around the country, including in Los Angeles. This time, Rick had a lot of overtime. Once, he was placed on an A/B watch, meaning he worked 12 hours on and then 12 hours off until eternity.

Okay, okay. It means until the end of a city emergency in Los Angeles.

Rick went to his night shift without a complaint and, honestly, without mentioning what happened at work most days. Due to all the negativity on the news, I tried not to watch it. But some days, I would put it on at night after our boys went to sleep. I saw protestors throwing things at police. The police stood there in their riot gear like statutes, not responding. Even though I did not see Rick, I saw him. You know what I mean, right?

The next chance Rick and I had time together without our boys with us, I asked him about the riots. I asked him if he had things thrown at him like I saw on TV. He said, "Yeah." Curious, I asked, "What did they throw?" He told me they threw Molotov cocktails and frozen water bottles and said they were told not to do anything in return.

Too many officers were being fired or sent to prison during that heightened BLM time.

I was facing BLM supporters in our community and my work. On Facebook, many fellow university faculty wrote "fuck the police" posts. I started unfollowing them one by one. The last straw was an email from our Faculty Union that stated, "white silence is violence," emphasizing that all faculty needed to voice our support for BLM.

I found myself alone in my experience amongst my colleagues and in our neighborhood. Many neighbors put up BLM signs in their yards and windows.

I stopped going on Facebook. I stopped attending any faculty meetings that were not required.

I looked out for a niche community of people who knew what I was going through, including some neighbors and friends who either empathized with police or had police officers in their families. Thankfully, I found comfort there.

Police Hate Prayer

Lord, soften my heart as I read and hear hateful comments about my police husband's profession. As I see or hear each negative comment, it is like a slap in the face. Remind me that they do not know. They are ignorant of the everyday challenges my husband faces. Soften my emotion. Let me be loving and not defensive. Empower me with assertiveness and confidence to state my opinion and love for my husband and all officers. Give me the wisdom to voice my opinion only when others are open to listening so that I do not exhaust myself trying with an audience that is not open to hearing what I have to say. Surround me with a community that respects and loves my family, including my husband's profession.

39. Motherhood VII- Choosing a School

James 1:17

Every good and perfect gift is from above, coming down from the Father of the heavenly lights, who does not change like shifting shadows.

A School that Felt Like Home

Maverick turned five years old in 2020 and was supposed to start Kindergarten that fall. Rick and I are a tad obsessed with education and did many kindergarten tours. One school stood out to us more than the rest.

During the school visit, we were invited to bring our children. Specifically, the school administration told us to bring our whole family. They said that choosing a school was a family decision. This was unique because many other schools we toured asked us to come alone without Maverick.

The tour began with a family chapel, which is how the school day always began. The Head of School did "call-outs" where he would say something, and the students would respond immediately in unison. There was a structure to the chapel format, and how the Head of School interacted with the students that felt almost militarized and familiar. The school administrators described it as a classical school. They believed in building followers of Jesus, who were critical thinkers. The school was what it was and did not try to appeal to each audience. It either was for you, or it was not. The school's vibe and values felt like Rick. It felt like home.

When Rick was home with our boys, there was more structure to our home than when it was just me solo parenting.

The tour ended with two gift bags for our boys and time to play on the school playground. Leonidas loved that part!

When we were interviewed by the Head of School, I told Rick that I thought I failed. I do not speak the Christian lingo because I was not raised in the church. The Head of School asked us where we worked. When Rick said he was a police officer, it did not phase the Head of School at all. In fact, he said that there were many other police and firefighter dads at the school already. We ended up being waitlisted for the school, confirming my fears. I prayed, asking God for Maverick to get into that school. He did get accepted before the school year started. Maverick started school at a place that already felt home to us. It was comforting in a time of chaos.

Prayer

Lord, I pray that my children learn in a place that makes them happy. I pray that you bless my children with a safe place to learn that shares our values and does not falter or change based on trends. I also pray that my husband and I are teachers in partnership with other teachers in our children's lives.

40. The Toe that Broke the Kristen's Back

About a year after Rick fully recovered from back surgery, he broke his baby toe at wrestling class. I told him that I was pretty sure our wedding vows included a clause that said he was only allowed to get injured once every 5 years in our marriage. Can I get an amen?

Prayer

Lord, I want you to know that the ending to that last story was a joke. I was there for him, but man, did I roast him for it. Who breaks their baby toe? Okay, I will stop joking about it now.

41. Finding Peace II

A Psalm of David 23:1

He makes me lie down in green pastures.
He leads me beside still waters.
He restores my soul.
He leads me in paths of righteousness for his
name's sake.

Big Sur

In addition to getting away to the cabin we
bought in Shaver Lake about a year after our first
visit there, we have been camping. Recently, we
went to Big Sur. We camped in a tent for two
nights. Rick was in his element. He put up the
tent, kept the fire going, and cooked most of the
food. That might be because when he left me
unsupervised for one minute, I tried to make a
wildfire! Seriously, a small fire started, but luckily,
Rick was nearby to contain it. Our boys had a
blast exploring around the campsite and a nearby
beach. We also went on a hike to a waterfall.
Rick said on our last night there, "I could live
here." I clarified, "You mean, like, in the tent?"
He confirmed, "Yeah."

It occurred to me that Rick finds peace in nature even though I just heard from a coworker of his that he is "a real good street cop" in the city of Los Angeles. It is quiet, and there is hardly any crime. You will find us out in nature more in the future to balance out the effects of his work.

Prayer

Thank you for making the mountains, rivers, and ocean. Jesus, I pray to ask for a day in nature when my husband or I feel overwhelmed. Please allow the greenery, running river or ocean water, and all-natural Vitamin C from the sun to heal wounds we have endured in this often-challenging life. Let us remember that we can be healed with time and patience from each injury or pain through love, prayer, and a quick escape to the mountains or beach.

Conclusion

In 2021 when I looked for a community that supported my family, I found you, other police wives on Instagram. I posted funny short-form Reels videos as @heelsandholster about police wife life to relieve my own stress during that time, and you laughed. I told you stories like the ones in this book, and you responded, "I feel seen." Little did you know that you made me feel seen too. Thank you for relating, laughing, and helping me feel less alone. We are all a part of a huge, thin blue line family.

My wish for you is that you find peace and joy in this life as it is a beautiful life. Our marriages to our hero husbands are worth the work it may take to find contentment and joy. Thank you for your family's service and sacrifices.

Peace be with you.

Other Resources

Visit www.heelsandholster.com for blogs with police wife resources and free police wife printables.

Complementary to this devotional, listen to "Be a Happy Police Wife in Motherhood" on Audible written by Kristen Linton, a 10-day practical guide to overcoming resentment and loneliness as a police wife.

Follow @heelsandholster on Instagram and other social media.

Made in the USA
Monee, IL
14 May 2023